Expected But Not Taught

Book 1: Technical Presentations

By Yvonne Ng

TABLE OF CONTENTS

Forward: Why I Wrote This Series

I actually wanted to call this series, *Everything I Meant to Tell You*. Why? Because this series is the accumulation of what I shared or wanted to share with my students at St. Catherine University.

Previous to teaching at St. Kate's (as it was affectionately called), I had worked in industry. Specifically, I worked in a consulting company where I was dropped into factories to figure out why their systems weren't working, or to design new systems for them that would link various parts of their company together: inventory, lab, weighing stations, storage machines, product developers, compliance, and even quality control.

I loved working in industry. Despite the warnings I was given as a woman engineer that factories were bastions of male chauvinism, I found my time at the factories to be some of my favorite moments. I also loved consulting. I would have to walk in to a new factory, figure out what everyone did with respect to the data, and then figure out what the tool should do and look like so they could do their jobs better or more easily.

It involved group brainstorming, problem solving, role playing, and a lot of empathy — putting myself into someone else's shoes. I also learned about powers of persuasion because despite the developer's belief that the new creation will make everything better, most people — from the factory floor to the research lab — really dislike change.

If more women knew about this, I thought, they would really like working in engineering and technology. If students knew more about this, then they would be better prepared — they would know that being a good employee would be more than just delivering quality code.

So, I went into teaching. I really wanted to share what I had learned and loved with students. To get them prepared and psyched about being savvy computer experts.

I started my teaching experience with night classes. These consisted of non-traditional students, usually older folks working a day job and wanting to change careers. For them, my experience in the industry was valued because I could tell them why they were learning about loops and conditional. I warned them about what to watch out for when stepping through arrays if you were working with not-so-careful languages (like C) that would let you step right into garbage memory locations, or worse, your own program.

Then, I was offered the opportunity to teach at St. Kate's. Since presenting "the real world" to women was a motivator for me to go into teaching, it made sense for me to take it.

My first class consisted of 15 women. Though smaller than my normal 25-30 student classes, the number of female faces staring back at me was at first disconcerting. Normally, there were only two women in the crowd, with one usually in the front of the classroom and one trying to hide in the back.

I can't tell you how odd it felt to have so many women asking questions about the intricacies of programming. It recommitted me to sharing as much as I could with the students. I wanted to not only make them competent, but successful.

The first year, I taught in very much the same way I taught at co-ed institutions — albeit a clearer, more active and visual way, than I was taught, but still pretty much focused on programming concepts. As the years went on, I realized I needed to help students learn how to act like professionals.

Part of doing that meant I needed to put students in situations that felt like "real life." Lectures became projects, which then required students to learn presentation skills and project management basics.

Later, I found I needed to provide team and professional development lessons so they could actually work effectively with each other and become "job ready." Students came out of their first computer course (CS1) with three projects under their belt (one of which was a 2-part team project), experience doing technical presentations to end-users, and the start of an interview portfolio. Many of these exercises and stories come directly from these lessons.

Since leaving teaching, I re-entered industry as a Business Systems Analyst. My years of teaching experience made me quite the expert in setting up project descriptions so the student could be successful. This is pretty much what I do as an analyst.

However, I have come to realize that the basic professional skills I taught students in college are not consistently known by those working in the industry. So in the hopes of helping our future IT workforce, I'm compiling these lessons from my classes along coupled with my experience as an analyst.

Consider this just a starting point: A jump start for those still in school and an insider's guide for those starting their first job as a member of the workforce. Because apparently, though these skills are expected at work, they still aren't taught in school.

Why Technical Presentations?

A lot of people are scared of presentations, but giving them are an essential part of work in industry, even as a computer or engineering professional. The presentation may just be a meeting with many other people or it may be more formal like what they make you do at school or a TED talk.

While a general "public speaking" communications class can teach you the basics of giving a presentation, there are some specific things about technical presentations which are unknown to those instructors. These are what I share with you in this book.

What Do You Need to Know About Technical Presentations?

In Brief:
Technical presentations are done all the time in industry. It is the easiest way to communicate progress, ask for decisions, and tap into team expertise.

When preparing a presentation, you need to know:
1. What your audience needs to know
2. What you want your audience to do as a result of your presentation
3. What your audience needs to see
4. How you can make it as easy as possible for your audience to listen carefully and understand so they can do what you need them to do

Public speaking is considered by many to be the scariest thing they ever have to do in their lives. As a computer or engineering professional, you will have to do presentations at least informally as part of a team. If you plan to advance or even own your own company, you definitely will need to make presentations.

If you can give short pithy presentations, you will rise

above the others because no one likes to spend their day in long meetings. Ideally, meeting time is informative and productive to so all attendees are up-to-date and on-board.

Presentations are sometimes made to a small group where participants have various expertise. They need to understand quickly what others are doing and what they need to do to interface with their work: Programming and electrical folks need to decide if the problem should be solved in hardware or software. Mechanical folks need to know about electrical decisions that will affect them.

Sometimes a slightly larger meeting is needed because marketing and sales need to be involved to be sure that the features being added make sense to the customer. They may also want to be sure the product stays within reasonable cost constraints and that the basic requirements are met. Sometimes it is a very large meeting when the big wigs (management, CEOs, etc.) need to be brought up to speed.

Why Are Technical Presentations Difficult?

In Brief:
Even if you took public speaking classes or did debate, technical presentations require you to explain technical problems and options to non-technical audiences so they can make key decisions.

Knowing how to do technical presentations helps in different stages of your life:
1. **College:** You will do well in class, independent study, capstone, or senior thesis projects which usually require presenting project results
2. **First job:** Your interview is like a mini-presentation, and some interviewers require you to do a short presentation. On the job, you will stand out as someone who can succinctly explain your contribution and how that fits into the larger context
3. **Future jobs:** If you can communicate to groups of people well, the sky's the limit, whether that's tech manager, VP of Engineering or CTO, or CEO

Technical presentations have some nuances that differentiate them from the standard presentations you may have presented in high school English classes. In some ways, the expectations are similar as business presentations: Brief, visual, focused. However, the technical presenter faces an added challenge of how to condense a lot of technical information and problem solving into a short period of time and often, to a non-technical audience. Even if the audience is technical, their expertise may be different from the presenter's (e.g. electrical engineers presenting to mechanical or civil engineers).

Studies and surveys of working engineers and computer professionals show that there is a knowledge gap regarding presentations: Presentations are expected in the industry but are not taught much or at all in school. Professionals indicate that presentation skills are essential for doing their jobs better as well as getting ahead. Those who communicate better are listened to more, are noticed more, are asked for recommendations more, are remembered more, and as a result, are rewarded and promoted more.

How to do it

Recall the main purpose of your presentation is to communicate. This is accomplished largely through:
1. Presentation Slides:
    a. What your audience needs to know
    b. What you want your audience to do as a result of your presentation
    c. What your audience needs to see
2. Presentation Delivery:
    a. How you can make it as easy as possible for your audience to listen carefully and understand so they can do what you need them to do

Tip 1: Present for a Reason

When giving a status or final presentation, **know what decision or action must happen as a result of your information**.

In the classroom, you are demonstrating what you have accomplished or learned while doing the project so the professor can give you guidance on a successful project (status report) or so the professor can award a grade (final report).

In the working world, you are informing the audience about the status of the product or process so that a decision can be made such as keep going, stop, change directions, or make key decisions.

Tip 2: Plan for 1 Minute Per Slide

PowerPoint or similar overhead projected slide presentation is the industry standard. It's best to use this practice to your advantage.

Plan on spending 1 minute per each slide in order to estimate the length of your presentation. You should include the first slide in the count, even though it's just the title and last slide (usually Q&A slide). Some slides will take less than a minute, others slightly more. If you plan on talking a lot for one slide, be sure to allot the right amount of time for it.

The novice makes up the slides with all the information that seems important and usually ends up with 20 slides. This is a lot. In order to have maximum success in communicating, you cannot feel rushed.

Tip 3: Start With a Bare Bones 6-min Slide Presentation

You should be able to give a status or final presentation on a term-long (3 month) project in just 5-6 minutes. This may seem unfair since you spent so long on it, but remember, a presentation is a conversation, not a reality show. This is not the time to present the intimate details and drama in hammering out your final product.

Here are the slides you should have in your presentation:

1 Title

Product Title

Team member 1
Team member 2
Date
Presented for xxx Review

Content: This is where your title (usually a description of your project or program), a subtitle, and your team members' names go. Other useful information may be: the presentation date and the company you work for or the class you are in.

Purpose: You are trying to frame why the audience is here, what they will learn about, and why they should listen to you.

Use the subtitle to indicate whether this is a status (e.g. concept, design, or implementation review) or final presentation. It helps frame what feedback you expect from the audience and the state of the project's "doneness."

Comments: This slide should not take you long, and you can largely read this slide. It may also be good for each person to introduce/say their own names.

2 BLUF

The Bottom Line

We created an app that allows the user to
- scan products on the shelf
- find out what we charge for it
- purchase it from us with a click of a button

We recommend final testing and then release on Google Play.

Content: BLUF stands for "Bottom Line Up Front." The purpose is to state the essential information that a manager or professor needs to know about what you did and your degree of success. The term comes from the military "briefings." Watch a war movie when the mission is being explained. This gives you a good model for what the BLUF is all about.

The bottom line is 1-2 sentences of 1) what was completed and 2) what is recommended as next steps. It is framed so the decision makers know the purpose and punchline of your presentation.

Purpose: Unlike a good thriller, your goal is not to hold your audience in suspense. It is to lay everything out on the table as soon as possible so the participants see what you see and can make the decisions that only they can make. This is especially important when you are working in the industry where presentations are not "academic exercises" but efficient ways for experts on a project to convey essential information to decision makers.

Comments: Other example BLUF statements are:
- We created a bicycle-powered pump that can take water from a rain barrel and spray xx square feet of lawn and can be manufactured for $xx. *If marketing feels we can sell it at a reasonable margin, we recommend that the project be allowed to progress to the implementation stage and contract manufacturers contacted.*
- This program is a game that drills students on facts about the Cold War. *It is ready to be launched on a website and we are all set to tweet to all the middle school history networks we know about.*

The status statement indicates what should be done next. For example: *Ready to launch, Complete, Basic, Needs later launch date, Cannot be done*

3 What Was Required / Done

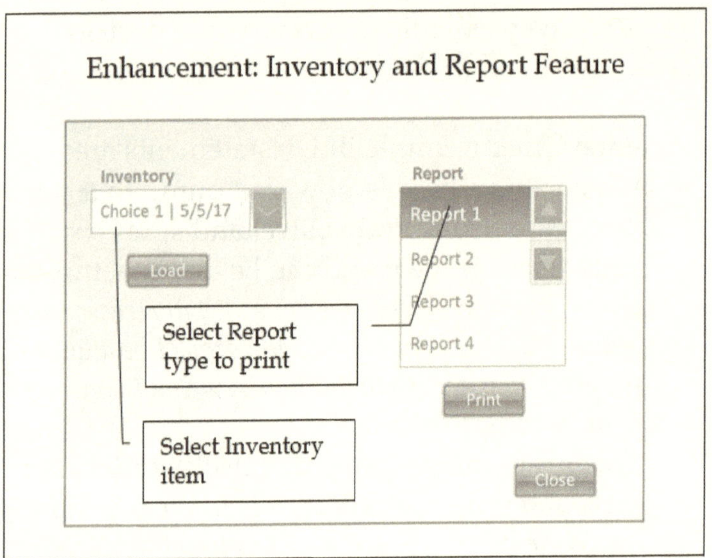

Content: For a course project, you should have received specifications ("spec") list for your project. These are the items that you MUST HAVE and probably some things that WOULD BE NICE. The MUST HAVEs are a priority, though some WOULD BE NICE may be easy to implement. These are called "low hanging fruit" so you might want to implement some of them first.

If you haven't been given an explicit list, be sure you make one up near the beginning of the project so your team is focused on how to prioritize work.

In industry, you definitely should have a specification or requirements list. This may be in the proposal that was accepted by the client, the Requirements document produced by the Business Analyst and signed off by the

Business owner, or the Key Design Features (KDF) document that was developed during kick off.

Do not underestimate the importance of this specification document. It is very important in industry to have this defined so that the client knows what is coming and the engineers/programmers know what to deliver. This keeps everything above board and communication clear on what is happening. It also prevents scope creep e.g. when the project to create a phone from off-the-shelf parts becomes a custom case with specially designed electronics!

Purpose: As a result, you need to clearly include these requirements in your presentation. The trick will be how to communicate that in just one slide. The best way to show that you have met specs is to have the current prototype there and demonstrate it or have a screen shot or program ready to show.

When presenting the status of your product, first address the MUST HAVE specs. Then show the features that you added. These are the WOULD BE NICE items or extra things that you put in to improve the quality or appeal of the product.

Comments: This is the time to stick with the facts. If you know how to fix a bug that prevents a key requirement from working, don't say that the requirement is satisfied. Keep this item for the next slide (see next section on *What Still Needs to Be Done*). Basically, if you say something works, you better be prepared to hand it over today, and the professor or client better be able to see that it works.

4 What Still Needs to Be Done

Limitations

- Constraints on the basic actions
- (Constraints on the features)

Content: Indicate the current limitations of the product in addition to items still on your to-do list. Limitations are the restrictions on the operation e.g. for one player, user must enter a number, device must be reset manually as it does not do so automatically.

If the limitation will be fixed before the final phase, indicate this clearly. If it will not, say so and give the reason why that is a good decision. Your professor or client may not agree with you, but give your recommendation and see what the final decision will be.

Purpose: Never hide the limitations of your product. You can try to spin it in the appropriate light, for example: *It is best to leave this limitation because of time, or money, or reliability.* But don't hide the fact that these limitations exist. Remember, you are working as a team with your managers, clients, and even professors. Everyone wants you to succeed, but they can't help you or make decisions that will help you if you don't present the true status. That is the reason you made this presentation.

5 Next Steps / Essential Questions / Lessons Learned / Future Projects

Essential Questions

- What is the best length for the lever?
- Which design option is preferred?
- Should the separate systems house their own rules or should there be a centralized rules engine?

Content: What you include in this fifth slide depends on your purpose:
- Reporting on status

- Presenting information for a decision

<u>Next Steps.</u> If you are giving a status report, use this slide to indicate your plans for future phase reviews. Show what you are planning to accomplish in the next phases. Explain how these milestones build to the final phase and product.

<u>Essential Questions.</u> In a status report, you may have questions that need to be answered in order to move to the next phase. This is the time to ask them because you have a wide range of experts, decision makers, and customers.

The questions can be *technical.* For example,
- We need to have it do xxx and are considering
    - Option 1: xx
    - Option 2: xx, or
    - Option 3xx
- Advice from the audience?

There could also be *cosmetic* questions. For example,
- What color is best for this?
    - We have narrowed it down to blue or green.
- Thoughts? Things to consider?

Sometimes a *key decision* needs to be made at this juncture. For example,
- In order to move ahead with prototyping, we need to purchase $xx,xxx worth of equipment.
- Is it appropriate for us to do so? Do we have permission to do so?

Note: In some cases, this might be the point when the upper management kills the project based on the information they saw in the previous slides. Your presentation should have contain the information they need to know in order to make this call.

Lessons Learned. In a class project, you can use this slide to tell the instructor and the class what you learned and overcame. When you interview, this will also be something valuable to include so companies can appreciate the extent of your experience. In a final presentation at work, it is valuable to share lessons learned with colleagues so if they run into a similar situation, they either know what to expect, have new ideas, or know you are a potential resource.

Future Projects. Ideas for future projects are usually presented in the final presentation. They are all the great ideas or features you came up while doing the project but just didn't have time to implement. Or they might be ways to refine your current solution in the future. It is always good to share the most compelling of these to instructors so they see your engagement in the project, but more importantly, you can show that you can make trade-off decisions to meet a deadline. It's good to share these in a work situation to show your engagement in the project and to get the audience (especially a customer) excited about the future potential of the project.

6 Q&A

Content: This slide is your concluding slide. It can have a single word on this slide "Questions?" It may also be useful to have a URL to your company website or demo version.

Purpose: This is where you orally thank the audience for attending and indicate that you are ready to field questions and welcome comments.

Tip 4: Design Slides for Maximum Impact

When I interned at NASA, one of the engineers said he couldn't attend my presentation, so could he look at my slides? He said, "I should be able to know what you're going to say from your slides."

I handed them over and warned him I had a different philosophy when it came to presentation slides: My slides are visual and minimal in words. I am an essential part of the entire presentation. I found later that my style was the more effective way and is expected in corporate environments.

Presentation slides should complement your oral presentation. The slides are also your "note cards" to trigger main points of your talk. They should never be read word-for-word unless there are just a few words on the slide (ones you want to emphasize). You are presenting on your project, after all, not showing the audience that you know how to read.

Studies have shown that using visual aids (pictures, diagrams, graphs) improve the effectiveness of talks by over 40% and the time required to give the talk is reduced up to 40%. Learning was shown to improve 200% if visuals were used.

The guiding principle of slide design is **"Less is more."** It is important to keep your slides short, not filled with words. The words that are on the slides should jog your memory of what to talk about rather than what to recite. Remember these guidelines:
- Maximum of 6-8 words/line
- Maximum of 6-8 lines/slide
- Use bulleted words, not complete sentences. You will talk about the details, examples, and specifics.
- Keep the visuals clear, clean, and simple

- Remember that actual objects are the best visuals. This is why a demonstration of your current product is expected.
- Use colors, but not more than 3 basic ones. Basic colors are blue, green, purple, and yellow. Remember that green may be seen as brown to those who are color-blind.
- Do a final check by asking yourself, your team, and / or a friend these questions about your slides:
    - Can my audience quickly and easily grasp what they see?
    - Is each visual truly enhancing my presentation or am I hiding behind it, using it as a crutch?

Tip 5: Consider a Handout

Handouts are not a normal requirement of presentations in engineering or computer science class settings, but they are often expected in the industry. This is especially important if there are no slides. Since many technical folks are visual people, a handout helps them see what you see. It also provides them something to "take away" if they need to remember what the presentation was about.

Normally, a handout contains the main points of your presentation but is not a direct copy of your presentation slides. The format of a page is different than the format of slides.

When creating your handout, imagine you are in sales.
If you have time (hah!), consider taking an introduction
to sales (sometimes a 2-credit class) to understand the
priorities of a salesperson. Otherwise, watch movies
about sales folks… there are more of them than about
engineers. One of my favorites for novices is *Big*.
Because the main character must learn about the sales
and marketing realm quickly, you can see a lot of the
ideas put into a nutshell.

The audience usually looks at the handout at the
beginning before you start talking, at the end after your
talk, perhaps during Q&A, and any down time during
the talk. Ask yourself:
- What do I want them to see at a glance? This is
  usually what they should know about talk going
  in and will see first when they skim the handout.
- What do I want them to remember? For when
  they read the handout at the end.
- What do I want them to take away with them?
  For when they read the handout after the talk —
  maybe when they talk about it with their
  colleagues, saying how great the talk was.

Remember that "A picture is worth 1000 words." Since
you are restricted on space ("real estate"), a well-
crafted picture or two might help you communicate
more effectively.

Although you have complete freedom in determining
what to put in your handout, there are a few specific
things I told students to follow these guidelines:

- Stick to **one page**. This can include front and back, but it is even better if you can keep it to one side as well.
- Have a title on the handout. This immediately frames the presentation for your audience.
- Include your team members' names
- Have a visual of your product—current, projected, or both—as appropriate for the type of presentation you are giving. This gives your audience a "sneak preview" of your product. Use callouts to show key features you will be talking about.
- Have a clear list of the questions you will need your audience to address (what you need them to contribute to the conversation)

Asking for feedback: Though your audience came to your presentation to learn from you, you may want to learn from your audience. I had students include a space for feedback so they could improve their presentation skills. The evaluation portion should be easy to detach from the handout so the audience members could take the handout with them. Here is a basic feedback form my students made:

Your feedback is appreciated!

PRESENTATION   Excellent-Good-Emerging-Needs Work-Poor
What did well:
What could improve:

PRODUCT   Excellent-Good-Emerging-Needs Work-Poor
What did well:
What could improve:

In industry, you may want to poll the audience about your product, especially if you will have a lot of people and some may be very quiet. For example,

Your feedback is appreciated!

PRODUCT
What was the most compelling feature:
What causes you the greatest concern:

Tip 6: Determine the Setup

In order to determine the best way to present your information is to first determine
- the space you will present in
- the equipment you will have

In particular, you want to determine the following well before the presentation:
- ***Where will the presentation be?*** Is it in a classroom? A lecture hall? In a gym? The size of the space will be important when determining your visuals, props for demonstrations, and voice control. Will there be a microphone? When possible, get into the room you will be presenting in prior to speaking. This way you can get a sense of the layout and where the audience will be with respect to you.

- *Can you use slides?* If so, be sure to follow Tips 1-4 when preparing your slides. If not, think about whether you can have a demonstration of your product (engineers) or posterboard representation of your screens (computer scientists).

- *What is the time limit?* You always want to stay within the time limit, or even a little below to allow for "questions & answers" which may include comments. If you are speaking as a team, you will need to plan and coordinate your content and timing so that one person does not take time away from another. Think about lectures that you have gone to when the professor runs out of time and doesn't complete the problem. Did you get irritated when the professor waved his or her hands and said, "Well, the rest is trivial; you can figure it out"? If so, you want to be sure that you don't do that to your audience. If you are a student, this is even more important because the professor will not be able to see all that you did.

- *Who will be in the audience?* In a classroom situation, will it just be the professor? Will all members of the class be there? Will there be other professors? Outside guests? Will the people attending know this material? Will they be technical? Do they represent the client or customer? How many people will be there? Knowing this will give you a sense of the language to use and the reasons why they are coming. See Tip 7 for more on this.

- *What is the interaction expectation?* How will you be interacting with this audience? Is it up to you? Will you do your full presentation and all questions will be held until the end? Will the audience ask questions as they arise during the presentation? If it is not specified, you can tell the audience how you would like to run the presentation when you start. It is always best to set this up beforehand rather than cut someone off in the middle. Of course, even if you say hold all questions until the end, someone may still ask a question. Sometimes it's just to clarify what you just said. You can even invite the audience to ask a question in the middle if they are confused, but in general, to please hold all questions to the end. The compromise on your end is to make your presentation as brief and direct as possible (see Tips 1-4).
- *Are there any other expectations?* Sometimes technical professors have expectations that they have not articulated. If so, be sure to ask them before the presentation about things you need to know to give your best performance. For example, I gave students the following expectations for the four presentations during the term:

1st talk: Personal Web Page
Audience: Professor
Time Limit: 5 minutes
Expectations:
  - Your client will be standing up with you.

He/she will give a short statement (not part of 5 minutes) about his/her satisfaction with your project.
- Professor will interrupt you at times.
- You may be asked to show where in the code a certain feature is defined
- You may be asked to make a modification to your code on the fly

2nd talk: JavaScript Project
Audience: Professor and CS Class
Time Limit: 5 minutes
Expectations:
- You can have a classmate "drive" the computer for you
- Introduce the members (explain any new members)
- Remember this is the final phase. Explain what the final product does and what can now be done with it
- You will be asked to enter new information to demonstrate that your program works properly. These will be within the stated limitations.
- You will be asked to list constructs you used and to provide examples of where you used them (e.g. I/O, variables, conditionals, etc.).
- Professor may interrupt you throughout your talk
- You may be asked to show where in the code a certain feature is defined

- You may be asked to make a modification to your code on the fly

3rd talk: Final Project – Phase 1
Audience: Professor, CS Class, guest professors/staff
Time Limit: 10 minutes
Expectations:
- Team will be presenting together
- Introduce the team members
- Each person speaks for equal amount of time
- No one should "drive" and talk at the same time
- Assume the audience is ignorant of the project and general programming
- The Q&A are handled relatively equally among all team members
- There may be some interruptions, but most questions will be held until the end
- If you anticipate a new team member in the next talk, prepare the audience for that

4th talk: Final project – Final Phase
Audience: Professor, CS Class, guest professors/staff
Time Limit: 10 minutes
Expectations:
- *Same as 3rd talk but with following additions*
- It would be polite to give formal thanks to the audience for their time and expertise.

- *What will be your delivery technique?* If you are presenting in a team, expect to do a trade-off where each person speaks and hands off to the next speaker. When two people are presenting, you could decide who will do which sections, or you could have one person present a main concept and the other commenting or expanding on that. Then flip it: the second presents while the other comments. It will need coordination but could make you look like a really cohesive team if you do it well.

Tip 7: Know Your Audience and Purpose

One mistake made in preparing presentations is to think only of the content. In reality, the content falls out when you know the audience. In a way, presentations are just another form of acting: there is a stage, an audience, and a message to convey. This chapter will break down the first two elements and the next chapter will address the message.

Remember in a talk that your purpose is to make sure the people in the audience get the message they should. That greatly narrows down the range of folks you have to communicate with from infinity to a much smaller number. Consider the following:

- Who is in the audience?
- Why are they here?
- Why might they be interested in this talk?

- What do I want them to get out of this talk? This is the most important to articulate as these are your **main points**.

When thinking about how to adapt or tune your speech for your audience so you achieve your main purpose, consider:

- *What devices can I use in the introduction to gain attention?* Examples can be pictures, jokes, stories, questions.
- *What steps can I take to relate this topic directly to the audience in the introductory slides?* This relationship should be clear to the audience by the time you start talking about your product in more detail (the third slide at the latest).
- *How can I develop these main points for* **this** *audience?* You don't have to make the best presentation for a generic audience. If your entire audience is going to be filled with engineering professionals, then focus on what is best to communicate with them.
- *What are appropriate supporting materials for this audience? What should be eliminated or kept in reserve for Q&A?* One common mistake novice technical presenters make is to include reams of codes, technical drawings, or calculations in their main body of slides. By doing so, you make it necessary to explain them in detail to those who understand it (most engineers can't ignore a blue print), or you confuse, intimidate, or alienate a person unfamiliar with that mode of communication.

- The experienced presenter does have key slides of this nature **after** the Q&A in case someone asks for details. Then you have the visuals that you need to delve into the technical aspects of the question, but you gave the main gist (**bottom line**) in the main talk for those who need to see the big picture.
  - In a class situation, you are usually asked overly technical questions for two main reasons: 1) the professor (or guest) is trying to evaluate your technical understanding of the topic or 2) there is genuine (geeky) interest in the problems you solved. Well, I guess there is the fact that the professor may be trying to stump you or put you on the spot, but that's really the dark side of reason #1, so just take it as something more innocent for your own mental health.
- *What special steps can I take to make my language clear and appropriate to this audience?* Ask yourself if, when you talk about the work you did, do you use technical jargon like "BOM", "prototype", "stress analysis", "HTML", "GUI", "compile", "applet"? The fact that you feel comfortable with these terms now shows how much you have learned, but remember that your audience may not know them like the back of their hand. If the term is important to use, then be considerate and either briefly define or explain it or ask them to be sure they do understand the term before continuing

to use it. Think about lectures where the professor used terms that you didn't know and how that affected your ability to pay attention and follow the lecture. Try to make your presentation the best possible learning environment for your audience.

Tip 8: Refine Your Delivery to Be Heard

Content and consideration of your audience are your primary concerns when preparing a talk. You should always have a desired purpose to your presentation. However, you can achieve this purpose better if you can give a masterful delivery. An effective delivery can engage the audience so they listen to you better.

It's tricky, though. Nervous or artificial speech may distract the audience to think about the *person* rather than the *information*. It is best to have a friend watch you make your presentation and give you feedback on which of these items you should work on.

Prioritize! Work on the most distracting item first. Improve on the other items each successive time you present. If you try to fix everything at once, you will likely fix nothing and make the existing problems worse by spending so much of your attention to them.

Voluntarily put yourself into a situation where you can practice speaking and presentation (e.g. volunteer work, Toastmasters, tutoring). It really does improve with practice, and there is no short cut.

Some common distracting habits are:

Eye Contact
- *What it is:* Looking at people. Not staring or talking to the screen or monitor
- *Strategies to improve:*
    o Move your eyes around the room to individual members of the audience. In particular, "give" a sentence or two to each member in the room If necessary, plant "friendly faces" (your classmates) around the room so you move your eyes naturally to each one and feel as though you are talking directly with them.
    o Position yourself so that you can see the screen and audience easily. This is often at an angle, to one side of the screen.
    o If you have a speaking partner, have one person "drive" the computer while the other talks. The "driver" advances the slides as needed, brings up the program to demonstrate, and presses the appropriate buttons/enters text to support the speaker. If the presentation computer is on one side of the screen (e.g. the left), position yourself so that you (the speaker) is on the opposite side of the screen (e.g. the right) so you can survey

the whole room and the driver. This keeps you, the speaker, focused on the whole room rather than always looking over your shoulder to tell the driver to advance to the next slide.

- *Benefits:* Good eye contact
    - Makes the audience feel important
    - Creates visual bonding
    - Lets you gather non-verbal feedback to let you know if the audience is understanding, is engaged, or is confused
    - Increases speaker credibility. In Western society especially, it is important to face the person (people) you are speaking to. If you don't, you give the impression of lying, not being confident, or not being trustworthy
    - Keeps the audience interested. Again, in Western society, eye contact is interpreted as engaging
    - Makes audience members feel talked to, as people
- *Cautions:*
    - Don't stare at any one person
    - Be aware that in different cultural settings, you may need to adjust your eye contact

Body Language

- *What it is:* This includes posture, gesture, and facial expressions

☑ **Posture**

- *What it is:* This is how you stand and present your body as a whole
- *Strategies to improve:*
    - o Stand up straight
    - o Open joints and limbs (take up space, sometimes known as "power stances"). This includes putting hands on hips, stretching out to point out something on the screen, etc
    - o Look forward, not down
- *Benefits:*
    - o Conveys self-confidence, professionalism, and credibility
    - o Helps breathing (which keeps you calm)
- *Cautions:*
    - o Watch bouncing back and forth, swaying and tapping

☑ Gestures

- *What it is:* This is what you do with your hands
- *Strategies to improve:*
    - o Keep them natural
    - o If what you do draws attention to your hands (people keep watching them rather than listen to you) – bad!
    - o If what you do reinforces content (e.g. explaining how things are placed, emphasizing a number of points) – good!
- *Benefits:*
    - o Helps you relax
    - o Helps audience relax
    - o Helps you emphasize what you are saying / main points you are making

- *Cautions:*
    - Stiff gestures may appear rehearsed
    - Too many gestures may be distracting if your audience finds them more engaging that what you are saying

☑ Facial Expressions
- *What it is:* This is what your facial muscles do
- *Strategies to improve:*
    - Relax your facial muscles before the talk: Wash your face with warm water, give your face a massage, tense all your facial muscles (eyes, cheeks, mouth) really tight and hold until you can't anymore. Then wash your face or give yourself a massage (or both) to relax
    - Tell yourself a joke or sing yourself a song in front of the mirror so you can smile naturally. Know what that feels like inside so you can know when you are relaxed during the presentation
    - Smile naturally
    - If someone is asking a question or commenting, allow yourself to show interest and attention that comes from listening (see **Tip 10: Manage Your Q&A**)
- *Benefits:* A relaxed face
    - Makes it easier to smile, respond to the audience, and talk clearly
    - Helps create a natural mode of conversation
    - Helps with voice control
- *Cautions:*

o Don't look bored or disinterested
o Don't overemphasize your facial expression which can make it look unnatural and artificial

☑ **Voice**
- *What it is:* The volume, rate, pitch, and pauses of your speaking as well as the clarity of your speaking
- *Strategies to improve:*
    o Vary the rate of delivery. Speak through some simple sections quickly, then slow down on areas you want to emphasize or that might be confusing.
    o Talk loudly enough for everyone to hear. Ask at the beginning of the talk if the farthest person can hear you
    o Talk with the audience, not at them. Be conversational, not lecturing
    o Show enthusiasm
    o Think "energy" – reaching out, not folding into self-contemplation
    o Articulate your words clearly. Don't mumble
    o Make sure your audience understands technical or unusual phrases
- *Benefits:* Good voice control
    o Gives a sense of natural speech
    o Keeps folks on track because they can hear you and the lack of monotony keeps them alert
    o Helps audience understand your message

- *Cautions:*
    - o Do not speak too fast or too slow
    - o Avoid talking too rapidly
    - o Avoid "ums" and "uhs". If you need a moment, take it. Pause for a moment to think about what you are going to say before you say it. Don't feel you need to "fill the space" with sound. Actors call this a "pregnant pause," and it can be very valuable in focusing both you and the audience. Sometimes a gesture, touching your lips with your finger or tilting the head to show that you're thinking may help. Try to avoid crossing your arms and wrinkling your brow as that often communicates that you are judging them and also disapproving of the question or topic.

Super Tip! If you really want to master controlling and reading body language, consider classes in sign language. Some schools offer it as a way to satisfy language requirements as well. Ballroom dancing is also a way to learn about body language (and apparently for men to meet women). Theater or singing classes can also help you control your voice, a great way to satisfy fine arts requirements. I learned body control and observation of body language doing tai chi and sparring.

Tip 9: Perfect the Little Things

Giving engaging and informative presentations is only part of being a professional. The little things not only count, but they can help you do your job better and more easily. Consider these when putting on those "professional touches":

Appearance

What you wear and how you appear are easy ways for you to improve your professional aura. Easy ways to do this are:

☑ **Dress**
Unless otherwise stated, you should dress Business Casual, at a minimum.

The rule of thumb is to always dress one level higher than your everyday dress. This shows that you recognize that this is a special event, not your normal work day. Also, by dressing up, you remind yourself to behave in a more professional manner. This means:

- No jeans, T-shirts, or shorts
- Button down shirt or modestly cut top
- Keep accessories (e.g. rings, jewelry) to a minimum

☑ **Teeth**
Teeth can be very distracting if not handled properly. If you have your audience engaged, they will look at you, and often, that gaze will fall on your face. With your mouth right there on your face, your teeth will have

front stage. When people meet you in person, your teeth will also be on display. Some tips on having them look their best:

- Brush at least twice a day. Consider brushing just before the meeting or presentation.
- When lunching before the meeting or presentation, avoid smelly foods like garlic or onions (or keep some fennel seed or mint on hand to neutralize the smell)
- Floss. This single action eliminates about 90% of mouth odor
- Check in the mirror just before meeting and look for food stuck in your teeth (e.g. spinach, pepper, beans, or lettuce)
- Chewing mint or fruit-flavored gum is a fast way to clean out your breath, but remember to throw it out before the presentation or meeting starts. Chewing or snapping gum is not a way to appear professional.

☑ Preparation

Presentation technology is helpful but also a risk factor. Some tips to mitigate that risk:

- Check your equipment (projector, computer with projector, microphone) well before the presentation, if possible. Definitely test it on the same day just before the presentation (e.g. the hour before). With different video ports (VGA, HDMI in regular, mini or micro forms), you will want to be sure your computer can connect to the projection unit
- Have your equipment and presentation set up before the audience arrives. For a class

presentation, plan on setting up well before the class starts if possible. That way, you have class time to handle any unexpected bumps. You don't want to look panicked or unprepared when the audience arrives

- Have a backup (on CD, flash drive, on the Cloud). Never have just one copy
- You may want to bring your own computer in case the presentation computer breaks down or doesn't display properly

☑ Last Minute "Once Over"

Give yourself a "once-over" in the mirror before entering a meeting or even leaving the house, making sure you look like a confident, presentable professional. This ensures that you are ready even if you meet clients outside the meeting room.

Greeting Guests

First impressions count. Here are some ways you can start off on the right foot.

☑ Handshake

A professional handshake is essential for a good impression in the United States. It should be crisp, firm, and warm, not limp, effortless, or sweaty.

During cold and flu season, some are a little "hand-shy" but the handshake is still important. Wash your hands and carry hand sanitizer with you if you are particularly worried.

If you are sick yourself (or recovering), then say so politely ("I'd shake your hands, but I think I may have a cold and really would not want to make you sick") and be engaging in other ways (e.g. "But I'm really glad you could make it" or "It's so great you could come out in such nasty weather"). See section below on **Small Talk**.

Shake hands when
- Saying hello or goodbye
- Before meeting starts
- When running into the person outside the meeting

Elements of a good handshake include:
- Offering your hand to shake (don't wait around for someone to hold out their hand)
- Clasping palm to palm ("web-to-web" is the general rule, referring to the web between the thumb and index finger of your hand touching the web of the other person)
- Look the person in the eye (again, eye contact is considered good in Western culture)
- Smile
- Match the other person's grip, but don't try to outdo them. This is not a competition. No arm wrestling matches
- Be firm but not forceful which would make the other person uncomfortable. Firmness conveys confidence in Western society
- Give the hand one or two good pumps (up and down) and then release

- If you are seated, stand up and shake. Staying
  seated communicates disinterest or passiveness.
  If you have a disability or are balancing
  something that makes rising difficult, state that
  and follow up with a good handshake (e.g. "I'm
  sorry, my cast makes it difficult to get up [hold
  out your hand], but I'm glad to meet you.")

☑ Introductions

When you meet someone for the first time, introduce
yourself. Don't wait around to be introduced.

When in a group, introduce those you know to each
other (e.g. "Sally, have you met George?"). If possible,
give a statement about the person on why the other
person should be interested in them (e.g. "George is
from XYZ company and is visiting today" or "I met
George during ABC project where he was the
electronics consultant").

If someone introduces himself/herself to you,
immediately repeat the person's name in your reply's
first sentence, it will help you remember the name.
Keep using it occasionally during the conversation (e.g.
"Nice to meet you, John" or "As John mentioned, we
needed to be aware of the customer's needs").

When there is a person you want to show respect to,
introduce that person first. In the case of customers or
clients, introduce them first (e.g. If Jones is the client,
say "Ms. Jones, I would like you to meet my partner,

Katie College. Katie, this is Ms. Jones, the President of
ABC Company").

☑ Recovery – Oops, What's That Person's Name?
If you forget a person's name, admit it (e.g. "I
apologize. I've forgotten your name" or "I have your
name on the tip of my tongue but can't seem to
remember it").

Don't avoid introductions to cover up the fact that you
have forgotten someone's name. Not introducing
someone makes them feel uncomfortable or forgotten.

☑ Small Talk
Sometimes it is necessary for you to mix with
customers before the meeting starts. Being able to do
"small talk" is a good way to fill this time. Here are
some ways to get started:
- Volunteer information about self or identify
  common interests, hobbies, or acquaintances
  (e.g. "Did you say you are from Harper's Ferry?
  I visited there when I was walking the
  Appalachian Trail.")
- Talk about the weather or weather-related items
  (e.g. "How have you been holding up in this
  heat?", "Can you believe the roads? I had a
  rough time getting out of my driveway this
  morning" or "I saw a crazy accident today.
  Ended up with a car in a tree!" — Actually, I saw
  a car in a tree on the way to work one day, but it
  wasn't weather related. It made a good small
  talk topic for a number of years.)

- Avoid controversial or off-color remarks (e.g. jokes about the weather are safer than those about religion, politics, or sex)
- Do not monopolize the conversation. Ask questions, listen, and appear interested (even if you are not). Allow some pregnant pauses as well. There doesn't have to be continual talking. A few quiet moments with a serene face may be just what everyone needs

Remember that you don't need to know exactly what you should do all the time. If you behave respectfully with the best of intentions, modifying them as you learn more, your efforts will be recognized and appreciated.

Using Feedback

Being able to handle and use feedback are ways to really improve professionally, especially when you get the feedback from folks you wish to emulate. However, it's sometimes difficult to take feedback. Many people focus on the negative ones, even if there are a lot of positive statements.

I require students to create feedback forms for audiences (see **Tip 5: Consider a Handout**). This helps them both improve and learn how to ask for feedback.

Some tips on reading and analyzing feedback:
- It's easier to take feedback if you wait a while after the event. Then you can approach it more objectively

- Before reading the feedback from others, try to give yourself feedback first. Write down the top 3 things you did well and the top 3 things you feel you could improve. By self-disclosing areas you know you need to improve, you will better consider the suggestions from others
- Separate the feedback into different areas. The primary ones to consider related to *What* you are saying (content) and *How effective* you are in communicating that
- Separate the feedback into
    - Those you know already (those in your self-disclosed "need to improve" list)
    - Those you hadn't thought of at all
    - Those you thought were fine (possibly in your "did well" list)

    Hopefully most of your feedback will be in the first two categories. If a lot are in the third, you may need to work with someone to recalibrate your understanding of the material, presentation, or delivery expectations
- Realize that you can't address everything and that not everything should be addressed. Try to select three specific things to improve for your next presentation:
    - Something that is easy to do
    - Something that you know you must work on
    - Something that may take a while to improve but you know you will mature greatly if you address it

Tip 10: Manage Your Q&A

The end of any presentation is the time for the audience to ask questions and for the speaker to answer them (hence the Q&A). You should know how to both ask questions and answer them.

The **ability to ask questions** of a speaker 1) helps clarify what you heard, 2) shows you were listening, and 3) often communicates appreciation to the speaker. It's actually very sad when a speaker comes to the end of the presentation and there are no questions or comments. I actually tell classmates to work with each other to have questions ready in case the guests don't have any. This allows everyone to practices asking questions and makes sure at least one question is asked so the presenting team can show their ability to answer questions.

The **ability to answer questions** 1) helps clarify what you were trying to communicate, 2) allows for exchange of ideas and perspectives, and 3) engages the audience in other aspects of the topic that may not have been directly covered in the formal presentation.

The following describe more tips on improving your ability to give an effective Q&A session.

Listening
First, become a good listener. You can do this in every class you take and meeting you attend. The key is becoming an active listener. Some guidelines are:

☑ **Focus**

This means getting focused on listening to your speaker. Tips include:

- **Work at actually listening.** Avoid the "entertainment syndrome" where you assume the speaker is supposed to entertain you. Think about professors you have had. Sure, some may have been entertaining, but did you learn what you needed to from all of them? Think about some boring professors. Sure, they were boring, but did some of them convey information clearly?

- **Reduce or eliminate sources of distraction.** If you are uncomfortable (e.g. in an uncomfortable chair, can't see or hear, too hot or cold), change the situation to make yourself more comfortable so you can listen (e.g. move to another chair or location, put on a sweater, adjust the thermostat or open a window or door). If there is a lot of external noise (e.g. coughing, noise in the hallway), take action to eliminate or mitigate it (e.g. offer a cough drop or glass of water, close the door). On the other hand, don't be a "finicky cat" — too much adjustment can be distracting to others. For adjustments that will affect others, look around to see if others are uncomfortable (e.g. sweating, hugging themselves to keep warm, leaning forward to hear). In these cases, speak up politely and propose a solution (e.g. "I'm so sorry to interrupt. I'm quite hot. Does anyone mind if I open a window?"). Do this only once or you *will* be a finicky cat!

- **Avoid daydreaming.** Some folks take notes to stay on task or doodle or knit. See tip on **Process** below.

☑ Mindset

This means getting into the right frame of mind to listen to the content. Tips include:

- **Mentally summarize what the speaker says.** Do this throughout the talk. It gives you a brief break from listening (e.g. "The speaker is saying that this may not be a cost-effective approach")
- **Keep an open mind.** Assume there is value in what the speaker is saying and how the problem was approached. Delay judgments until you fully understand the intention and content that the speaker is communicating
- **Recognize your own biases.** This can include how you solved the problem (e.g. distracting biases are "Why did they solve it that way? We did it this way, and it's so much better"). Realize how these biases may influence what you hear
- **Avoid selective listening.** Selective listening is hearing only what reflects your own attitudes and believes or what you did or learned in your project. Avoid filtering out difficult messages. It can prevent you from learning something new from another person's experiences

☑ Process

These are some processes you can do to keep your listening active:

- **Judge content as delivered, not delivery as**

content. While you as a speaker need to pay attention to the little details of your presentation like body language, you as a listener need to avoid attending to the nonverbal aspects of the message if they overwhelm the content of the talk (e.g. fidgety or nervous speaker, poorly designed slides). Communication is a two-way street, and you as a listener have a role in making yourself an effective receiver of the information, despite any poor delivery. As engineers and computer scientists, we will run into our fair share (or more than our fair share) of poor lecturers, but we have to learn as much content as we can from them. Don't dismiss the speaker's expertise based only on his or her speaking ability. Do your best to understand the main points and evaluate those

- **Look for key ideas.** This is similar to the idea of summarizing what the speaker says (see **Focus** tip above)
- **Take notes.** The act of taking notes helps many do the above

Caution! Beware of oversimplification. This is the elimination of details to simplify complex messages so they are easier to remember. You will be dealing with very complex systems as you progress through your technical career. Learn how to capture the big picture and organize the complexity in an understandable way without losing essential details. This is a transferrable skill as well: folks in business, finance, and even public policy need to be able to do this. I personally try to turn the speaker's words into pictures or process flows.

Thinking on Your Feet

Now that you are a good listener, it's time to think about the Q&A as a speaker. The trickiest part of Q&A is that you don't know what someone will ask. You will need to "think on your feet." Here are some steps on how to answer questions on the fly gracefully:

☑ **Listen**

Look at the person. Pay attention to what he or she is saying. Do not think about what to answer before you hear the entire question.

☑ **Pause**

Use a moment to organize your thoughts. A moment of silence is okay. Breathe. Some folks lay a fingertip on their mouth to show they are processing and thinking about the question. It is important to take some time to organize your thoughts and recall appropriate information needed to respond.

☑ **Repeat question or summarize question**

When you do this, you ensure that you understand the question correctly. Sometimes the asker doesn't quite know how to ask what is on his or her mind, so your rephrasing the question into something you feel you can answer can help. Nick in *Zootopia* phrased this well: "The secret to a press conference is to ask a question and then answer it."

☑ **Clarify the question.** Sometimes, though, you aren't sure what is being asked. A few ways to clarify the question are:

- **Ask to have the question repeated.** Extroverted folks process as they speak, so the first time through, they may have been working their question through and when asked to repeat it, they can summarize it better. Ways to do this are "I'm not sure I understand the question completely. Can you repeat it or rephrase it?" or if you have a good rapport with the audience, "Can you say that again, but differently?"
- **Propose a clarification.** State what you think the person may be asking (e.g. "Are you asking…" and insert what you think the person is asking here)
- **Ask for a definition.** If the person uses a term you're not sure of, ask for a definition. It will be essential that you are both using the same definition to give a good answer (e.g. "When you ask about 'cost effective,' are you wanting to know what the investor will earn versus invest or are you wanting to know about the long-term maintenance costs and revenue expectations?")
- **Clarify or define a point yourself.** If you think you understand what is being asked, but you have to assume a few things, restate a clearer question and see if that helps (e.g. with the examples above, "If you are asking … *a question you feel is better defined and you can answer accurately*, then the answer is …" or "Assuming 'cost effective' is evaluated in the first 3 years of the products' life, the profits will pay for all initial development costs and annual maintenance by that time and earn $xx,xxx annually thereafter")

☑ **Respond rather than answer.** This is important in a meaty question like the "cost effective" one above. Answering the question requires a lot of processing, calculations, and logic, so the temptation is to go through the processing, calculations, and logic. If you do this, though, you may end up giving a whole new speech, which is not appropriate in a Q&A setting.

Instead, give one main item, ideally the **bottom line** to that question (see **Tip 3: Start with a Bare Bones 6-min Slide Presentation**) and then *stop*. The audience will ask if they want to know more or want you to walk them through in more detail. You can even offer to go through in more detail, but say you're not sure if that's what they really want to hear or focus on at this time.

For example, you could respond: "There are a few different ways to evaluate 'cost-effective'. If the product is sold at a retail prices of $xx per unit, then all initial development costs and annual maintenance will be recouped in 3 years and earn $xx,xxx annually thereafter. However, if you are thinking of a different criteria, is this something that you would like to discuss now or after the talk?"

- **Stop.** When you have said what you have to say to answer the question, then stop. Dragging on is not effective and may discourage others from feeling they can ask their questions. Also, don't end on an excuse or the phrase "I don't know" or "I guess." If you don't know how to end, summarize your main point with one sentence (e.g. "That's why we did …").

Good Manners

Answering questions is a time when you can speak as yourself and not from a prepared talk. It can be a great time to show yourself as a real professional. This is most easily done by using good manners with all you contact.

☑ As a Member of the Audience

As a member of the audience, you should:

- **Clap** at the end of the presentation. It may be awkward if you find yourself the only one clapping to start, but keep going. Others will join in if you don't falter, and if you were the speaker, you would appreciate it. On the other hand, don't clap too early! The best time is when the speaker says he or she is now ready for questions. If possible, preface it with a statement "First, thank for your talk" or others may think there isn't time for questions. If questions start right away, then when Q&A is done, try to do a thank you and initiate clapping
- **Provide feedback** through oral questions, written comments, or citing interesting points or ideas presented, especially if they give you insight into your own work. Opening phrases to do this include:
    - "I really enjoyed your talk. I have a question about …"

- o "You mentioned *this* in your talk. Can you talk a bit more about that, especially as it relates to … *something you are working on and would like insight on*"
  - o "I appreciate your mentioning … It's very similar to what I'm working on with …"

Student Tip! If you're in a small class (5-25 students), consider doing the second item frequently. It creates good rapport in the class and gives you practice at making comments or asking questions. Regarding the clapping, when I was at Princeton, it was typical to clap at the end of the final lecture to show appreciation for the work the professors did during the term. Sadly, this was usually done more in large lecture halls so a lot of technical professors (who taught in rather small classrooms) didn't get the applause. Technical professors need love, too!

☑ **As a Speaker to an Audience**

As a speaker, it is good manners to

- **Greet the audience** when they arrive. See above sections on Introductions (in **Tip 9: Perfect the Little Things**)
- **Inquire about the audience.** What are their interests, experiences, relevant background? Why are they attending today? You can ask informally before the talk or if it's important for framing your talk and time permits, you can do at the beginning, before or after your own introduction. If you know more about the audience, you may be able to relate their

interests to your talk better with this
information.
- **Thank them for coming.** Give thanks at the end,
  just before opening up to Q&A. This also tells
  your audience that you are done. And if they are
  polite themselves, they will clap then.

☑ As a member of a team

If you are presenting as part of a team project, you
should show good manners to your teammates as well:
- **Trade off speaking** when possible to show that
  you all have shared responsibilities and
  accountability to each other
- **Thank them** if you are helped by them. This is
  done during the presentation as well as before
  and after the presentation. It can be as simple as
  thanking the driver for switching the slides,
  holding the door, or helping a teammate carry
  their stuff
- **Complement them** if they do a good job. This
  can be done during the presentation (e.g.
  "Thanks so much, Jane, for setting the stage for
  why cost is an issue… I will now present the
  financial analysis") or when you feel they did a
  great job during the project (e.g. "Ashley did
  some great analysis for that question and I can
  walk you through them now").

Tip 11: Develop a Healthy Presentation Perspective

Who would have guessed there was so much involved in just delivering a good presentation? Some folks who are uncomfortable with speaking can get worked up and even negative about the process.

Developing a good perspective about presenting, questions, answers, feedback, and such makes it easier to become a professional. These are some guidelines I gave students as well as new professionals when it seems like every meeting is a mini-presentation:

Questions are Good
These include questions from you, to you, and for you. Don't cringe when they are asked and don't be afraid to ask them.

Evaluate Intentions
I won't lie to you. Questions are asked for a variety of reasons:

- **A sincere desire to understand** the topic more
- **An attempt to challenge** you to see the depths of your understanding (most usual in a classroom setting or interview). It is an assessment strategy, not a belligerent attack.
- **A desire to antagonize you.** If the person does not outright say antagonistic things such as "You're an idiot" or "You don't know what you are talking about" or "You are talking garbage"

then assume that the intention is one of the first two items. Often, in a technical environment, the asker may be trying to understand but lacks the sophistication of doing so in a polite way. Thus, you should treat as bullet #1: "a sincere design to understand" and not get offended or defensive. Doing so gains you points in the eyes of others who usually will know if the asker is "challenged" in how to ask questions politely.

If you suspect the person may actually be antagonistic (there are a few), ignore it and treat it more like the first two. Clarifying is a way to "neutralize" the aggressive question (e.g. "Are you asking to learn more about … *topic being discussed*" or "Are you wondering what my experiences is with … *this topic* …? If so … *describe your experience, expertise, etc.*"). We live in a civilized society so others will see you are able to remain graceful under fire. However, if you find these suspiciously antagonistic questions from many during an interview, you may want to decide whether you want to be in a community where that will comprise normal interactions.

It's a Conversation, Not a Quiz
Don't get test anxiety. Unlike a test, if you don't understand what's being asked, you *can* clarify the question. That's not cheating; it's being a good conversationalist.

Don't Go Off Track
Answer the question that is being asked. If you must go off track to give background, details, or special

considerations to answer the question accurately, always acknowledge that before you start (e.g. "Before I answer that, let me be sure to emphasize that we need to first remember … *important background to consider*").

By giving this "heads up," you allow your asker to clarify his or her question, prepare for a long answer, or withdraw the question. You've seen that before, the person may respond, "Well, it's probably off topic. We can chat about it offline."

If you do find yourself off track, come back as soon as you can to the original question. Restate the original question to be clear that you are now answering it and then answer it. Then stop.

Have fun
Presentations at school prepare you for meetings at work, and if they are done well, they can be highly productive events. And you get to know the folks you work with and create a great rapport.

All of my students actually like giving presentations by the end of class. They find it fun after doing many meetings and presentations with their now familiar group of classmates. You will find this familiarity gives you insight into the nature of your classmates, colleagues, customers. You can smile about little jokes, personal tidbits, and general human connections you have discovered, and this human understanding can creep in to normal interactions can make the work day more pleasant—and you get the job done, which is always a plus, too.

The *Expected But Not Taught* Series

So ends this "primer" for Technical Presentations. Presenting is one of the skills that is expected of you as a professional but not explicitly taught. Now that you know how to improve your presentation skills, the next thing to do is to practice. It is okay to feel a little anxious before giving a presentation. Use this pang of insecurity to motivate your preparation and rehearsal. It's best not to get too cocky no matter how many you have presented successfully.

I made students do four presentations in one 14-week term in my engineering and computer science courses. All the students said that presenting was no longer a problem for them by the end. In fact, some really enjoyed it.

If you identify skills required for your computing or engineering professional success are not taught in school (e.g. project and team skills), don't give up. As they say in *GI Joe*, knowing is half the battle. The other half is figuring out how to fill that gap.

First, look for good professor or TA who can develop and mentor you. Look in your internship company for a mentor. Or maybe you have a relative who can help.

In case you don't have any of those, this *Expected But*

Not Taught series will hopefully point you in the right direction.

Other Useful Resources

If you want to see briefing examples, peek at
- The You Tube video "B-17 & B-24 Bombing Missions: 'Target for Today' 1944 US Army Air Forces Training Film World War II" at about 30 minutes in
- The Death Star briefing in *Star Wars*
- Mission descriptions in any TV or movie *Mission: Impossible*
- *The Dirty Dozen* introduction of the mission

Presentation and communication in general is well researched. Here are some of my go-to books.

Campbell, Clark A. and Campbell, Mick. (2012). *The new one page project manager.* Hoboken, NJ: Wiley.
- Essentials in project management communication to gauge time, people, tasks – and feelings!

Donaldson, Kristin. (2005). *The engineering student survival guide.* NY: McGraw-Hill.
- Dense book of tips for the engineering student with section on presentations.

Beer, David and McMurray, David. (2005). *A guide to writing as an engineer.* Hoboken, NJ: John Wiley & Sons, Inc.
- A good book for general writing tips. There is a small chapter on presentations which touches on preparing, delivering, and listening to presentations.

Foster, Timothy R V (2002). *Better business writing.*

London: Kogan Page Limited.
  - Great book on how to keep writing succinct and focused in a professional settings, including emails and overhead (presentation) slides. Nice demonstration of how slide content is related to what is said, though I would suggest informative visuals when possible.

Frank, Milo O. (1986). *How to get your point across in 30 seconds or less*. NY: Simon and Schuster.
  - Classic in getting to the point. Important in writing and talks.

King, W.J. (original) and Skakoon, James G. (revisions) (2004). *The unwritten laws of engineering*. NY: ASME Press.
  - A must-have for any new engineer. Every time I pick it up, I remember why my engineering training helps me succeed in IT.

Selinger, Carl. (2004). *Stuff you don't learn in engineering school*. Hoboken, NJ: Wiley-IEEE Press.
  - Tips and exercises to help develop some of the non-technical skills expected of a professional

Volin, Kathryn J. (1999). *Buff and polish*. Virtualbookworm.com.
  - Good how-to book on developing presentation skills

Zobert, Justin. (1997). *Writing for computer science*. Singapore: Springer-Verlag Singapore pte Ltd.
  - Writing basics but put in a computing context

Who I am

Good critical thinking! You should wonder who I am in order to determine whether I am worth listening to.

What technical things I have done:
- Computing professor (13 years)
- Automation engineering consultant (5 years)
- Freelance computing consultant (2 years)
- Project engineer in product development consulting firm (2 years)
- Business systems analyst consultant (4 years and counting)

Relevant educational experience:
- Mechanical Aerospace Engineering undergraduate with emphasis in control systems (projects like a magnetic levitator and microprocessor controls)
- Mechanical Engineering graduate with
  - Graduate computer science minor
  - Thesis using C++ and object-oriented databases for solid modeling to evaluate STEP interface before it became an industry standard for CAD systems

Experience teaching computer technology and engineering:
- Taught CS1, CS2, computer architecture (using EE/Computer engineering approach and years of Heathkit electronic and assembly programming experience), graphics, data

structures and algorithms
- Advised numerous independent study projects
- Was control systems Teaching Assistant who conducted voluntary recitations (3 terms)
- Taught self-developed "engineering for everyone" course that eventually became introduction to engineering for engineering majors and required for all elementary teachers who were required to teach engineering in schools

Other things I did I feel worth mentioning:
- Mother, wife, business partner, author, toy designer